Montréal.

Cobblestone streets, centuries-old architecture, iconic markets. A little slice of Europe in North America. You've seen the movie. The sequel's better.

LOST iN takes you off script in a city where storytellers paint the skyline, bars hide skate bowls and subzero temperatures only turn up the heat. You'll uncover rooftop parties, roving raves, towering plant sculptures, decades-old drum circles, a Sex Pistols–inspired restaurant, a Shinjuku-style speakeasy and a literal underground art scene. This is the city beneath the city, and we're not talking about le RÉSO.

Along the way, meet the people making it happen: the adventure guide who pioneered St. Lawrence River surfing; the chef cooking up river-eel carbonara; the concert promoter holding the line for indie music; the street artist creating portals to other worlds; and the guitarist from Canada's first all-female death-metal band who traded riffs for gothic pet portraiture.

Eat weird, drink late and dance outside. That's the Montréal that exists beyond the Old World veneer. Get lost in the Montréal where the New World is taking over.

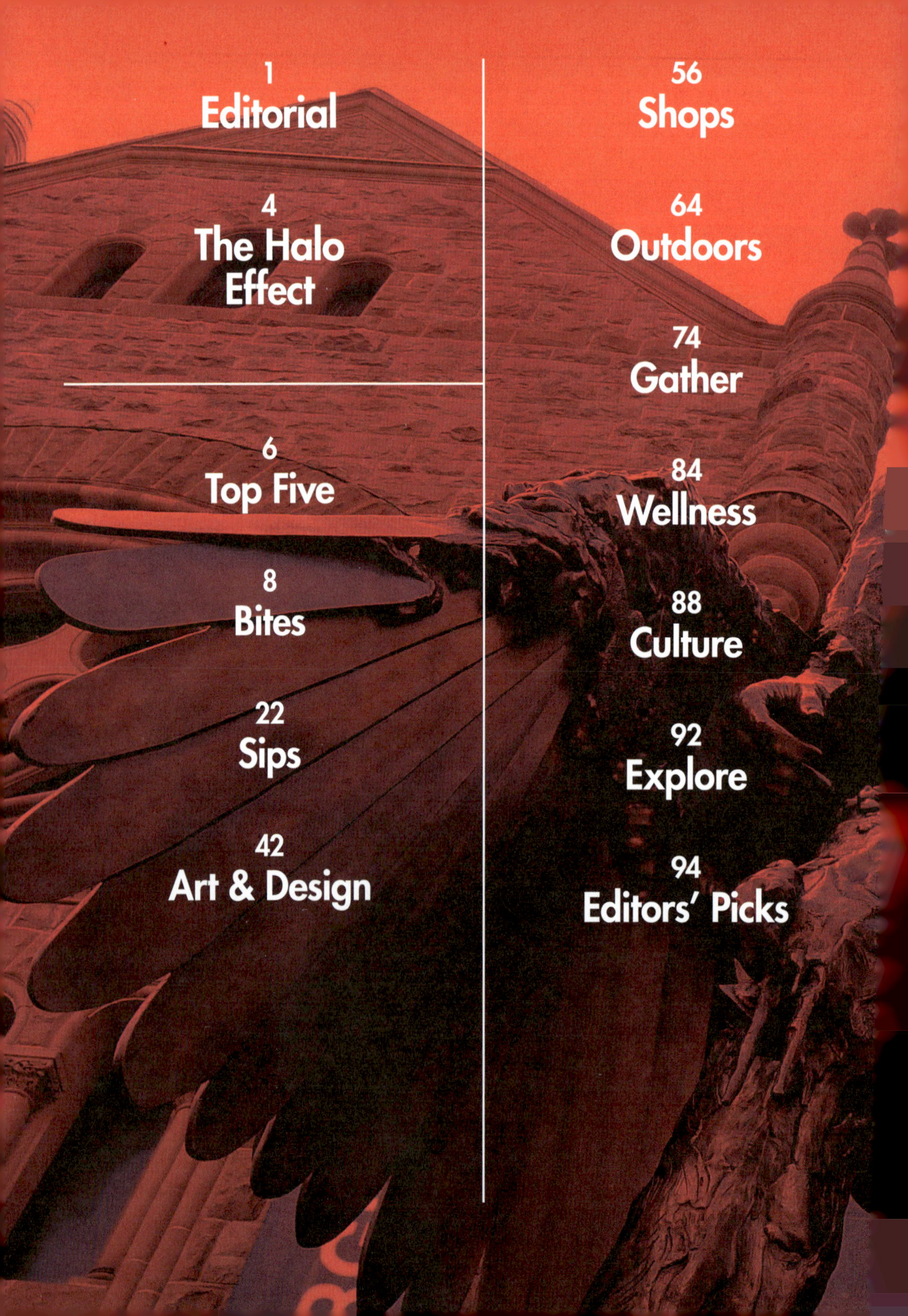

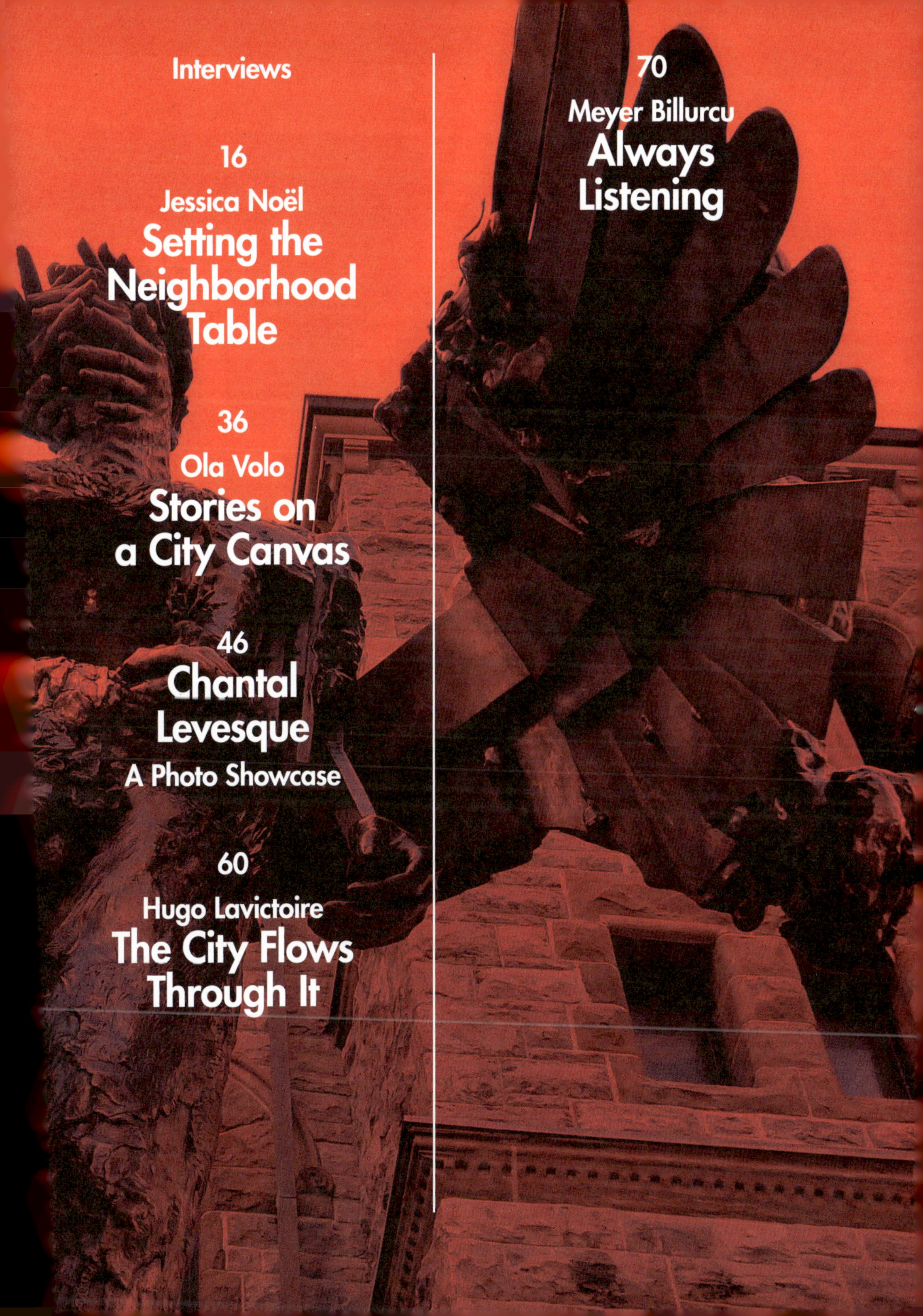

Interviews

NOUVEAU
CENTRE

The Halo Effect

At first glance, *The Ring* appears to be a giant steel halo suspended between the towers of Place Ville Marie, but it's more than an architectural statement. The 98-foot public artwork was designed to frame one of Montréal's most iconic views, perfectly aligning McGill College Avenue with the Mount Royal cross in the distance. Visit at sunset, when the reflecting pool doubles the spectacle.

• The Ring, Esplanade Place Ville Marie, Downtown

Photo: @jfsavaria/Tourisme Montréal

Top Five

The city's greatest hits. With a few deep cuts. Start spinning.

Coveted Tables

- ☐ Toqué
- ☐ Joe Beef
- ☐ Restaurant Beba
- ☐ Monarque
- ☐ Le Violon

The Art Circuit

- ☐ Blouin Division
- ☐ Bradley Ertaskiran
- ☐ Art Mûr
- ☐ PFOAC/Pierre-François Ouellette Art Contemporain
- ☐ Station 16

Vinyl Hunting

- ☐ Cheap Thrills
- ☐ Phonopolis
- ☐ Aux 33 Tours
- ☐ Sonorama
- ☐ 180g Café-Disquaire

Neighborhood Crawls

- ☐ Mile End
- ☐ Plateau Mont-Royal
- ☐ Old Montréal
- ☐ Little Italy
- ☐ Saint-Henri

Wall Artists

- ☐ Kevin Ledo
- ☐ Roadsworth
- ☐ Zilon
- ☐ Jason Botkin
- ☐ Bonar

Smoked Meats

- ☐ Delibees
- ☐ Schwartz's Deli
- ☐ Lester's Deli
- ☐ Snowdon Deli
- ☐ Dunn's Famous

Musical Landmarks

- ☐ Bar Le Ritz PDB
- ☐ Casa del Popolo
- ☐ Place des Arts
- ☐ Monument-National
- ☐ Leonard Cohen Mural

Go Vintage

- ☐ Eva B
- ☐ Marché Floh
- ☐ Citizen Vintage
- ☐ Annex Vintage
- ☐ Empire Exchange

Urban Green Space

- ☐ Parc du Mont-Royal
- ☐ Jean-Drapeau
- ☐ Parc La Fontaine
- ☐ Lachine Canal
- ☐ Parc Jarry

Poutine Gone Wild

- ☐ Ganadara: Korean bulgogi and kimchi
- ☐ Casserole Kreole: Haitian pork griot
- ☐ Ma Poule Mouillée: Portuguese mixed
- ☐ Au Pied de Cochon: French foie gras
- ☐ MajesThé: Japanese curry katsu

Plated Storytelling

From wood-fired bagels and smoked meat to Cambodian tapas and punk-rock tasting menus, Montréal doesn't do culinary boundaries. Pull up a chair and dig into a city where traditions get shaken up.

Photo: Patricia Brochu

Monkey Business

Les Street Monkeys serves up Cambodian tapas fusion designed for sharing. Wasabi shrimp ceviche, Phnom Penh–style bone marrow and other boundary-hopping dishes bring big flavor to every plate. The energy continues in the funky industrial interior, where orange, black and red set the mood. Meat and produce are sourced primarily from Montréal and nearby farms, including local mushrooms and chicken from Charlevoix. The inventive drinks menu rotates through creations like the Yuzu Snooze Yuzu Lose, made with Gin Trésor No. 13, amaretto, corossol and yuzu. Save room for the crème brûlée "of the moment."

• Les Street Monkeys, 3625 Wellington Street, Verdun, streetmonkeys.ca

Anarchy in the MTL

Cabaret l'Enfer answers the question, what if Sid Vicious became a chef? The result is fine dining rooted in punk rock, dark surrealism and old-school Parisian cabaret. We're talking Sex Pistols imagery, skull motifs, a loud soundtrack and a wild bathroom that demands selfies. Chef Massimo Piedimonte turns seasonal ingredients into edible art, layering color, flavor and theatrical flourishes. Named Canada's second-best new restaurant in 2023, Cabaret l'Enfer is one of the few Michelin mainstays that feels more like an underground London club than a fine-dining destination, which is exactly the point.

• Cabaret L'enfer, 4094 Rue Saint-Denis, Le Plateau-Mont-Royal, cabaretlenfer.com

Photos: Clara Lacasse, Bayrut/Tourisme Montréal

Gather Round

Bayrut channels the spirit of a Beirut family table, where sharing isn't just encouraged, it's expected. The menu travels across the Levant, from silky hummus and smoky *muttabal* to fragrant kibbeh, charcoal-grilled meats and freshly baked *manakish* flatbread emerging from the oven throughout the day. Portions are large, flavors are bright and over-ordering is practically a house rule. Come on a Tuesday for a quiet dinner or a Saturday to make a night of it: Bayrut handles both without breaking a sweat. Just make sure you save room for dessert.

• Bayrut, 727 William Street, Old Montréal, bayrut.ca

Repeater

Trattoria Fugazzi brings playful energy to Italian comfort food in this sit-down version of the local pizza brand. Wood-fired pizzas are the headliners, with creative toppings and names like the Notorious P.I.G. and Pikashew, but the pastas arguably share top billing. Take the cacio e pepe, made with fresh radiatori and truffle, flambéed with cognac and served inside a wheel of Grana Padano. There's also a three-course tasting menu, all-you-can-eat pasta on weekdays, and cheeky cocktails like Leave the Gun, Take the Cannoli. It's a menu you can't refuse.

• Trattoria Fugazzi, 1886 Rue du Centre, Pointe-Saint-Charles, fugazzimtl.com

Photo: Scott Usheroff/Tourisme Montréal

The Cool Uncle

Oncle Lee reimagines Chinese cuisine through a contemporary lens. The ever-evolving menu draws on regional Chinese traditions while embracing seasonal produce, resulting in colorful sharing plates that balance familiarity with surprise. Hot pot, seafood and noodle dishes get paired with a wine list that keeps up with the big flavors and clever cocktails, while the buzzy dining room strikes the perfect balance between neighborhood favorite and destination restaurant. Its newer sister restaurant, *Oncle Lee Kǎo* (photo), applies this same approach to the grill, firing up dishes like lamb skewers with cumin and shishito peppers.

• Oncle Lee, 222 Laurier Avenue West, Mile End, restaurantonclelee.com

Heat Wave

Pichai has fast become one of the city's most exciting tables, serving bold takes on Thai street food. Chef Jesse Mulder's menu brings together vibrant curries, charred meats and pristine seafood, layered with heat, acidity and fragrant herbs. Think tapioca dumplings stuffed with candied pork and peanuts (*sakoo sai moo*) and minced meat *laab ped* with grilled duck hearts. An open kitchen keeps the energy high, while natural wines and inventive cocktails complete the experience. Bring a crew, order generously and let the table do the traveling.

• Pichai, 5985 St-Hubert Street, La Petite-Patrie, pichai.biz

Send Noodles

There are no secrets in the *Nouilles de Lan Zhou* kitchen. Watch the chefs hand-pull noodles in the storefront window, putting on a show for shivering passersby on snowy winter days. Inside, there's usually a line, but rarely a long one: The no-frills menu and lightning-fast service mean bowls are ordered, served and slurped in record time. The beef and dan dan noodles are top picks, while a small but mighty side of spicy cucumber brings a kick of crunchy freshness. Add the perfectly tea-boiled egg to level up any bowl.

• Nouilles de Lan Zhou, 1006 Saint-Laurent Boulevard, Chinatown

Beautiful Mischief

One of Montréal's most stylish tapas spots, *La Bêtise* is chic without the attitude, with warm wood and soft lighting creating the perfect night-out glow. Nothing here is quite what you expect: a gin-based Unicorn Basil Smash shares the menu with quail egg mac and cheese, while standouts include salmon tartare, lamb dumplings and spicy fried cauliflower bites. Settle in for the full tasting menu or graze over drinks with friends—ideally on dollar oyster night, if you can catch it. With its playful, confident approach, the kitchen creates a memorable night out, one small plate at a time.

• La Bêtise, 3807 Wellington Street, Verdun, labetise.com/en/home

Photos: Audrey Eve Beauchamp, Christina Miranda/Touris

Pacific Crossing

Blending Japanese technique and bold Peruvian flavors, *Nikkei MTL* explores one of the world's most exciting fusion cuisines in a sleek setting. The menu moves effortlessly between minimalist nigiri and tangy potato *causas*, citrus-bright ceviches and crispy tostadas, each highlighting the natural overlap between the two culinary traditions. Cocktails follow the same cross-cultural approach, incorporating Japanese spirits alongside Peruvian ingredients and tropical accents. Whether you're stopping in for a drink at the bar or settling in for dinner, it's one of the city's most compelling destinations for modern Nikkei.

• Nikkei MTL, 1577 Laurier Avenue East, Plateau-Mont-Royal, nikkeimtl.com

Raw Precision

Tamisé Sushi brings a refined touch to neighborhood sushi dining. The menu revolves around impeccably prepared sashimi, nigiri, hosomaki and futomaki, while delicately torched sushi adds the smoky depth that quickly became a signature. Vegetable-forward rolls receive equal attention, with inventive combinations that stand comfortably on their own. Don't overlook the artisanal sauces, from heritage soy aged in cedar barrels to a yuzu-infused blend made by an 18th-generation brewer. Pair them with a sake or Japanese whisky, and let the evening slow down around you.

• Tamisé Sushi, 4721 Sainte-Catherine Street East, Mercier-Hochelaga-Maisonneuve, tamisesushi.ca

Photos: Tourisme Montréal, Christophe Roberge/ Tourisme Montréal

Rise & Dine

Lines out the door are nothing unusual at this beloved newcomer to Verdun's brunch scene. But what sets *Janine* apart isn't just the food, it's the warmth. On rainy days, staff hand out tea, baked goods and umbrellas to those waiting outside, a level of hospitality that carries through the entire experience. Guests are greeted with juice shots when they sit down, while homemade marshmallows floating atop hot chocolate have become a signature touch. Don't leave without ordering the Scotch egg, latkes or the classic *gros jambon* breakfast plate.

• Janine Café, 3900 Wellington Street, Verdun, janinecafe.ca

The Bagel Standard

For nearly 70 years, *St-Viateur* has been hand-rolling and wood-firing bagels for Montréal. Founded by Jewish immigrants in the late 1950s, this multigenerational family business makes a chewier, crispier alternative to New York's classic boiled bagel. Montréalers proudly carry St-Viateur tote bags, while cafés across the city serve its bagels, making a visit to the original location a rite of passage. Every bagel is made in-house and pulled hot from the wood-burning oven. Enjoy one with butter or flavored cream cheese, or fresh off the rack with nothing at all, just as the locals do.

• St–Viateur Bagel Shop, 263 Saint-Viateur Street West, Mile End, stviateurbagel.com

Fusion Fabulous

"Kwizinn" comes from the Haitian word for cuisine, and owners Michael Lafaille and Claudia Fiorelli opened this Old Montréal restaurant in 2017 to bring the flavors of the Caribbean to the city. Since then, *Kwizinn* has become a neighborhood favorite for hearty tasting platters and a vibey Haitian rum bar. Regulars come for comfort-food classics like Creole lamb and Barbancourt jerk ribs, while rotating events and group experiences add another reason to return. Think Tomahawk steak dinners for two and speakeasy-style tastings for up to 30 guests.

• Kwizinn Vieux-Montréal, 311 Saint-Paul Street East, Old Montréal, kwizinn.ca

Photo: Two Food Photographers

Morning Glory

Michael Tozzi opened *Dandy* in Old Montréal with an already impressive résumé, including a stint leading the kitchen at *Olive + Gourmando*, the buzzy café just a few blocks away. His own restaurant is bright, stylish and unapologetically indulgent, with a menu that embraces the best of breakfast-lunch crossover: fluffy ricotta pancakes, a buttermilk-fried chicken sandwich and smoked salmon toast topped with a poached egg and dill-pickle cream cheese. The all-natural wine list is joined by a cocktail menu of brunch classics, from mimosas and espresso martinis to Caesars, Canada's vodka-spiked answer to the Bloody Mary.

• Dandy, 244 Saint-Jacques Street, Old Montréal, dandymtl.com

Jessica Noël

Setting the Neighborhood Table

Few restaurants have shaped the country's culinary landscape quite like *Vin Mon Lapin*. Led by co-chefs Jessica Noël and Marc-Olivier Frappier, this Little Italy institution pairs produce-driven cooking with one of the city's most celebrated natural-wine programs. The team has since expanded its orbit with *Rôtisserie La Lune* and a seasonal cookbook, while the accolades keep stacking up. Vin Mon Lapin topped Canada's national restaurant rankings in 2024 and landed at No. 5 on North America's 50 Best Restaurants 2026—the highest showing for Eastern Canada. It's an "absolute cornerstone of the Montréal scene," as the Michelin guide put it. In other words, book early and often.

Vin Mon Lapin
Little Italy

Rôtisserie La Lune
La Petite-Patrie

Le Vin Papillon
Little Burgundy

The bistronomy movement in Paris has seen restaurants move away from white tablecloth formality and focus on market seasonality. Is that how you would describe Vin Mon Lapin?

I would say that's pretty accurate. In the beginning, we were looking to do a wine bar because we were part of the Joe Beef group with Marco [Frappier] and Vanya [Filipovic], the other partners. They had opened *Le Vin Papillon*, and then we opened this new place in the same line because it was in a different section of the city. We realized later on that our ambition was a more traditionally shaped restaurant.

Most restaurants with your level of acclaim only do tasting menus. Do you ever feel the pressure to go in that direction, or do you love being able to offer à la carte?

We love the freedom. We have a [tasting] option if people want us to choose for them, but keeping it more casual has been part of our success. We want people in the neighborhood to say, "I'll come and eat like two apps and have a glass of wine and go back home." We want both options: people who

Photo: Dominique Lafond

Jean-Talon Market
Little Italy

Le Violon
Little Italy

Bar Saint-Denis
Little Italy

Restaurant Limbo
Little Italy

go all out, and the regulars who want a quick snack.

You change up the menu a lot, but there are a few signatures. Everyone raves about the smoked eel carbonara, the scallop sandwich, the buckwheat and honey cake and the sourdough-crusted chicken.

The scallop sandwich has been there since 2022 and the buckwheat cake since the first day. They're always on the menu. The others are there when the moment allows. The smoked eel carbonara was on the first menu, but we can't always get the smoked eel.

The eels come from the St. Lawrence River?

Yeah, in the estuary, closer to a region called Rimouski. Right before the Gaspé Peninsula, the St. Lawrence widens up, so it's a river-meets-the-ocean section. It is the source of most of the seafood that we get. A lot of the urchins are from there. Even larger fish like halibut at the beginning of the season. It's one of our favorite places in Québec, and we have a great supplier there. We've had a relationship since we opened. They smoke the eels for us, and then we transform it in our own way afterward.

You're known for sourcing produce from local markets like Jean-Talon. *Do you physically go to the market yourself?*

This time of year, I go to the market practically every day, even if it's not to buy produce. Before our suppliers and farmers can tell

Bistrot Boisselet
Little Italy

St-Viateur Bagel
Mile End

Schwartz's Deli
Le Plateau-Mont-Royal

Snowdon Deli
Côte-des-Neiges

Smoked Meat Pete's
L'Île-Perrot

La Banquise
Le Plateau-Mont-Royal

Arthurs Nosh Bar
Saint-Henri

us something's available, small quantities sometimes pop up at the market. Or we can have a conversation at the market and ask, "When are fava beans coming?" It's a way to see what's coming and get inspired. A lot of the produce we get is from farms that don't have stands at the market itself. But some of the stuff does come from there, definitely. It's an inspiration.

The restaurant is famous for natural and low-intervention wines. For those who prefer standard wine, what experience at the restaurant might surprise them?

There's a stigma about natural wine with super-funky macerated situations that can be overwhelming, almost just by the smell. But there's such a wide range of what natural means, and it doesn't always have to be a funky wine. There are some very streamlined, delicious, more conventional-tasting natural wines. Everybody can find what they're looking for even if they're into more traditional wines.

Tell me about The Mon Lapin Cookbook: De Toute Beauté.

We really wanted to convey what a night in the restaurant can be. A lot of storytelling. Since we cook seasonally, everything is split up into how it presents itself to us during a year, and each chapter has a wine section allocated to it. We took care of all the recipes, but Mireille Silcoff wrote all the beautiful words for us. She has a great point of view that's not what you normally get from a cookbook author.

You opened Rôtisserie La Lune in 2024. Why chicken?

Two reasons. At Mon Lapin, we've always worked with smaller animals, and we love poultry. It's an ecological thing, but also a size constraint where we won't have whole beef carcasses coming in and no space in our walk-in fridge. On the other hand, there's a big tradition around rotisserie chicken in Montréal. There are big chains. You speak to anybody who grew up in the province, and they ate at Electric Chicken [before it closed].

You were a stagiaire *[trainee] at several iconic kitchens around the world. What did you learn?*

In culinary school, I applied for this scholarship and had three *stages* of three months. You always walk away with recipes that have an impact, but I got more from seeing how all these places function every day.

In Vienna, I was at Steirereck. The restaurant did traditional food and had their gastro side all mixed together in the same kitchen, which I thought was super interesting. Then I went to Frantzén [in Stockholm], which had just two [Michelin] stars at the time, and they were clearly striving for that third star. You could feel an energy, and I really loved to see everybody working towards the same goal. Then I got to Blue Hill at Stone Barns [in New York] and felt *this is my place*. I loved running about the chaos. There's so much produce, so many changes on the menus. I thrived in these situations more than in super-structured places that do the same thing every day. But I respect both sides.

We're happy that we've gotten to a point where our cooks have a nice lifestyle. Not everybody is stress-dreaming about having to be so precise or coming in with little rulers and tweezers. That's what I took away from all those *stages*, how I wanted to adapt myself in this restaurant.

Pichai
La Petite-Patrie

Beba
Verdun

Montréal Plaza
La Petite-Patrie

Pied de Cochon
Le Plateau-Mont-Royal

Joe Beef
Little Burgundy

Nora Gray
Griffintown

Gia
Saint-Henri

If somebody wants to understand Montréal through food, where should they go besides Vin Mon Lapin?

In Little Italy, here's *Le Violon*, *Bar Saint-Denis*, *Restaurant Limbo* and a new restaurant called *Bistrot Boisselet*. It's a classic French bistro vibe but with produce from small farms. You have to eat the bagels at *St-Viateur* and have the smoked meat at *Schwartz's* or at *Snowdon Deli* or outside of the city at *Smoked Meat Pete's*.

Poutine is a late-night food, and it's all they do at *La Banquise*. That's their cuisine all day, from quite early to very, very late. It's a sign of a fun night out if you end up eating poutine.

I think *Arthurs Nosh Bar* for a delicious brunch. We love *Pichai*. They do delicious Thai food with a super-nice list of natural wines. Walking through the markets will give you an idea of the ingredients in season, and it's a great place to people watch.

There's also the regular heavy-hitter if people are coming from out of town. If they come to see us, we often ask, "Where else are you going?" It's usually *Le Violon*, *Beba*, *Montréal Plaza*, *Pied de Cochon*, *Joe Beef*, *Nora Gray*, *Gia*. There are so many restaurants to explore in Montréal, in every neighborhood. Other than the food, the bigger highlight that always leaves a mark is the hospitality that is so unique to the city. Familiar, friendly, warm and so knowledgeable. It's the real star of the show.

What is your favorite neighborhood to explore with no plans?

My neighborhood, Little Italy. You're a stone's throw away from Jean-Talon Market. Saint-Laurent Boulevard has tons of little stores, shops, cafés and a great concentration of restaurants. All the Italian cafés have such a great vibe. You really feel like you're in a small neighborhood.

Be an elite wanderer
The Air Canada Aeroplan® Card
Experience something elite.
Learn more at Chase.com/AirCanadaCard
AIR CANADA AEROPLAN
CHASE
Mastercard, the circles design, World Mastercard and World Elite Mastercard are trademarks of Mastercard International Incorporated. Chase Air Canada Aeroplan Card credit cards are issued by JPMorgan Chase Bank, N.A. Member FDIC. Accounts subject to credit approval. Restrictions and limitations apply. Offer subject to change.

Sips

The Night Circuit

More than just serving great drinks, Montréal creates great nights. From curated wine lists and legendary pubs to inventive cocktails and inclusive sports bars, these are the places to raise a glass.

Photo: Lovedino/Karolina Jez/Tourisme Montréal

Waste Not

La Mal Nécessaire built its reputation on sustainability, using every part of the produce: juice for a drink, skin for a garnish and the outer shell for serving. Favorites include the Coco Supremo, served in a shaved coconut, and the Santiago Spritz, made with spiced purple corn. DJs spin house music on vinyl nearly every night, and the room offers a lively dance floor with soft leather chairs and booths tucked along the edges. Whichever you choose, the seductive lighting makes it easy to settle in for a long night.

• La Mal Nécessaire, 1015 Saint-Alexandre Street, Downtown, lemalnecessaire.com

Uncork & Unwind

A Michelin Bib Gourmand and a Wine Spectator Award of Excellence give *Annette bar à vin* plenty of credentials, but it wears them lightly. Tucked into Rosemont on Molson Street, it's the kind of neighborhood wine bar that pulls you in for one glass and keeps you for dinner. The draw is a thoughtful selection of low-intervention wines from independent producers, a short seasonal menu built around local Québec ingredients and a room that hums rather than buzzes. Come for a quick apéro, stay because the evening keeps finding reasons for another round.

• Annette bar à vin, 4051 Molson Street, Suite 120, Rosemont-La Petite-Patrie, annettebaravin.com

Timeless Taste

With throwback décor and impressive drinks, *Bar Dominion* has become a regular fixture on lists of Canada's best bars. Housed in a century-old space, it pairs classic tile and woodwork with Art Deco accents, while its knowledgeable staff is always ready with a smart drink recommendation. Order the seafood tower with a French 75, followed by steak tartare, and finish with a house-made churro. From the lighting to the service, everything feels timeless and inviting. It's easy to see why Bar Dominion, opened in 2023, quickly became a fixture of Montréal's cocktail scene.

• Bar Dominion, 1243 Metcalfe Street, Downtown, dominionmtl.com

Game On

A longtime queer bar in the Plateau, *Champs* mixes sports-bar energy with an events calendar as diverse as its crowd. Catch the "Habs" hockey games on the big screen, join a lesbian social night or dance through a weekend DJ set, then come back for free pool and themed trivia if you'd rather compete than dance. Located on Saint-Laurent, Champs is easy to reach and surrounded by the neighborhood's dynamic energy. Cheap drinks and an unpretentious crowd keep regulars coming back night after night.

• Bar Champs, 3956 Saint-Laurent Boulevard, Plateau-Mont-Royal, champsmontreal.com

Skate After Dark

It's one of Montréal's coolest after-dark hangouts. Think graffiti-filled dive bar with a soundtrack that leans heavily toward electronic and hip-hop, but the venue's biggest conversation starter is the full-sized skate bowl tucked inside the bar. According to the team behind *TRH-Bar*, it's the only club in the city where you can catch skaters (such as Raph Séguin in the photo) dropping in before heading out to the patio or dance floor. Loud, casual and proudly unpolished, it's a uniquely Montréal night out, where skate culture and nightlife collide under one roof.

• TRH-Bar, 3699 Saint-Laurent Boulevard, Plateau-Mont-Royal, trh-bar.com

Aperitivo Hour

Canada's first aperitivo bar, *Bar Bello* brought the Italian pre-dinner ritual to Montréal's Little Italy and hasn't looked back. The focus is on *amari*, vermouth and spritzes, with snacks and sharing plates that make it dangerously easy to turn one drink into three. There's real family history, too, as the Bello name has been part of Montréal's food scene since the late 1970s. Add warm lighting, an easygoing soundtrack and the buzz of Saint-Laurent, and you have the perfect setting for an evening that unfolds without anyone checking the time.

• Bar Bello, 6740 Saint-Laurent Boulevard, Little Italy, barbellomtl.com

Reach for the Stars

Climb a glow-in-the-dark staircase above a pizza joint, and you'll emerge in a room well worth the ascent. A tropical-plant-draped vaulted glass ceiling, neon-lit glass-brick walls and sweeping curves give *Milky Way Cocktail Bar* a retro-futurist personality that never overshadows the drinks. The ever-changing cocktail menu leans into seasonal ingredients and inventive techniques, resulting in complex drinks that are genuinely fun to drink. Even the playful names—One Last Drink, Monkey on a Break, and Boys Want Flowers Too—set the tone for the bar's anything-goes spirit.

• Milky Way Cocktail Bar, 1886 Centre Street, Pointe-Saint-Charles, milkywaycocktails.com

Sláinte!

Hurley's Irish Pub is a Montréal classic in the heart of downtown. With live Irish, rock and folk music every night, plus timeless pub fare, the bar pays tribute to the Irish immigrants who helped shape the city. It's an unpretentious, community-minded place where university students and 50-year regulars share pints side by side. While Crescent Street outside can be loud and chaotic, Hurley's stone walls and warm interior offer a cozy, enduring refuge. It's a reliable spot for a beer or cocktail any night of the week.

• Hurley's Irish Pub, 1225 Crescent Street, Downtown, hurleysirishpub.com

High Score

Montréal's first bar dedicated entirely to arcade and retro games, *Arcade MTL* has been running on pixels and microbrews since opening in 2016. Rows of classic cabinets and retro consoles are the draw, but the real appeal is the atmosphere: bright, social and genuinely fun in a way that has nothing to do with being a serious gamer. A small cover charge gets you unlimited free play, so grab a themed cocktail and challenge your friends to *Street Fighter*. Turns out competitive *Pac-Man* is an excellent icebreaker.

• Arcade MTL, 2031 Saint-Denis Street, Quartier Latin, @arcade_mtl

Hidden in Plain Sight

The hardest part isn't choosing a drink. It's finding the door. The payoff? A night that feels like an adventure before the first sip.

Down the Alley

Down a rather menacing graffiti-lined alley, this speakeasy bar hides an intimate, sophisticated interior behind its rough, red-bulb-lit exterior. *Atwater Cocktail Club* pours hundreds of spirits alongside adventurous dishes like escargot and frog legs, and its wildly photogenic bathroom has become an attraction in its own right. Cocktails with fun names like the Siren Song and the Pink Panther are crafted with unexpected ingredients ranging from pollen to blue cheese. Whether you're settling in for a long evening or just passing through, the surprises keep coming long after you've found the door.

• Atwater Cocktail Club, 512 Atwater Avenue, Saint-Henri, atwatercocktailclub.com

Bottle Service

Hidden behind an unassuming entrance on a major boulevard, *Big in Japan* has earned a cult following for its craft cocktails, Japanese whisky selection and candlelit atmosphere. The bar practices *botoru kīpu*, a Japanese tradition in which customers can purchase a bottle of whisky, have it stored at the bar and return to drink it over multiple visits. These personal bottles hang above the winding bar, creating a striking interior and a deeply personal drinking experience. With understated service and sexy lighting, it's one of Montréal's quintessential late-night escapes.

• Big in Japan, 4175 Saint-Laurent Boulevard, Plateau-Mont-Royal, @biginjapan_bar

Duck for Cover

Finding *The Coldroom* is part of the fun. Just follow the duck. That's the only hint the bar gives to its nondescript entrance, which descends into one of the city's best-kept drinking secrets. Inside, exposed brick, low ceilings and soft lighting set the scene, but the real draw is behind the bar: timeless classics and bespoke creations, mixed with the kind of confidence that doesn't need to announce itself. Order something classic, or tell the bartender what you're in the mood for and let them take it from there.

• The Coldroom, Saint-Vincent Street x Saint-Amable Street, Old Montréal, thecoldroommtl.com

Photo: Dominique Larond

The Perfect Fit

Hidden behind a tailor's shop, *Cloakroom Bar* seats just 25 and has no printed menu. Instead, bartenders open with a conversation—your preferred spirits, your flavor inclinations, your mood—then disappear behind the bar and return with something you didn't know you wanted. The result feels less like a night out and more like being welcomed into someone's very well-stocked private salon. Impeccable technique, an understated room and one of Canada's most impressive collections of vintage spirits make it one of the city's coolest places for a cocktail.

• Cloakroom Bar, 2175 De La Montagne Street, Golden Square Mile, cloakroombarmtl.com

Scenic Sips

Up for a Drink

Trade the street for the skyline. The higher you climb, the more Montréal unfolds beneath you, with views of the river, port and mountains.

Photos: William Gray/Daph&Nico/Tourisme Montréal; Two Food Photographers

High Spirits

Forget the downtown rooftop circuit: *Taverne Atlantic* in Mile End draws a crowd of locals, natural-wine drinkers and people who found the place through word of mouth and kept coming back. The drinks are anything but run-of-the-mill, with a craft beer list that might move from a local Messorem IPA on tap to a bottle of Cosmo Burdock ale aged on whole-cluster Cabernet Franc grape skins. The wine list is just as diverse and offbeat. Small plates, pizzas, cocktails, cider and vermouth round out the offering.

• Taverne Atlantic, 6512 Avenue du Parc, Mile End, taverneatlantic.com

Raise the Roof

Montréal's highest outdoor terrace sits 44 floors above Place Ville Marie, and *Rose Orange* makes the most of the altitude. The terrace opens onto sweeping views of the entire city—the St. Lawrence, Mount Royal and the street grid dissolving into the horizon—in a panorama that could justify the trip on its own. Early evening draws an aperitivo crowd, while DJs and cocktails shift the mood later without sacrificing the easygoing appeal. Seasonal drinks and Mediterranean-inspired sharing plates make the experience about more than just the view.

• Rose Orange, 1 Place Ville Marie, 44th floor, Downtown, roseorange.ca

Top Shelf

Hidden behind lush greenery on the ninth floor of the *Humaniti Hotel, Terrasse Alizé* feels like a secret garden stocked with cocktails and a barbecue. The menu ranges from small plates and salmon poke bowls to tacos, with flank steak coming off the grill from 5pm. It's heartier than the average rooftop offering, and all the more satisfying for it. Themed events, from Arabian Nights to Spritz Sundays, add a playful energy, while the leafy setting makes it equally appealing for a leisurely afternoon or a night out.

• Terrasse Alizé, 340 De La Gauchetière Street West, Old Montréal, terrassealize.ca

Photos: Tourisme Montréal, Terrasse Belvu Hors-Piste/Daph & Nico/Tourisme Montréal

Old-World Views

Perched above the 19th-century buildings that house *Hotel Nelligan, Terrasse Nelligan* has a strong claim to the best view in Old Montréal. The St. Lawrence River, Old Port rooftops and church spires unfold beneath you, a vista best enjoyed with something cold in hand. The menu keeps things classic with seasonal cocktails, wine, champagne and light bites, while the popular weekend mimosa brunch makes it just as tempting by day as it is at sunset. It's the kind of view that makes a quick drink feel like a very bad plan.

• Terrasse Nelligan, 106 St-Paul Street West, Old Montréal, hotelnelligan.com/nelligan-terrace

The Upper Deck

One of Montréal's largest rooftop terraces, *Muze* sits above the *HONEYROSE Hotel* with a pool, cabanas and egg-shaped hammock chairs that give it a decidedly resort-like feel. The menu covers salmon tartare, sharing plates and seasonal cocktails, while the panoramic views stretch across the city's rooftops and Mount Royal. As daylight fades, DJs take over and the atmosphere shifts into high gear, turning the terrace into one of Montréal's liveliest alfresco spots. It's a polished rooftop escape with just enough vacation energy to make the city feel far away.

• Muze Lounge & Terrasse, 355 De Maisonneuve Boulevard West, Quartier des Spectacles, muzemontreal.com

Photos: Adrian Williams/Tourisme Montréal, K Lee/Tourisme Montréal

Sea

Ola Volo

Stories on a City Canvas

Ola Volo is a Montréal-based muralist and illustrator from Kazakhstan whose work draws on the folklore traditions of her childhood to create large-scale narratives. Her paintings are populated by powerful female figures, mythological symbols and personal memories, woven together into compositions that read as complete stories without a single word. Her murals can be found across Montréal, Vancouver and beyond, and she's worked with clients like Apple, Lululemon and Louis Vuitton.

Your visual language blends Eastern European folklore, Kazakh storytelling traditions and West Coast nature. How do these different sources coexist in a single piece?

I was born and raised in Kazakhstan, so that part of my work has always been nostalgic. I moved to Canada when I was 10, right on the cusp of remembering everything from my childhood but no longer having access to it. When we moved to Vancouver, I encountered something completely new: a massive ocean, the Rockies, bears in our backyard almost every day. That unfamiliar world naturally made its way into the work, too. What drew me to Eastern European visual storytelling was the tradition of illustrated plates. I became obsessed with the idea that a piece could be visually complex and yet the eye could move through it and understand the story without any words. That fusion of East and West, past and present, is where I found myself as an artist.

Your work draws on folklore traditions from your upbringing. Which characters, symbols or stories do you find yourself returning to most often?

I create a lot of female characters. A woman representing other women is something I'm naturally drawn to. I think a lot about feminine power, about women who take up space. They're proud, empowered, almost glorious, often wearing a crown. And then within the pieces there are small personal details: fire, light, flowers, a moment from my grandmother's kitchen, the pattern on a little teapot she kept on the table. I know these women so well. Sometimes a character travels with me across different walls. She changes, but it's somehow the same woman. Sometimes I see myself in her. Sometimes I see my mother. I don't always know until I step back from a finished piece and think, *Of course, there she is.*

Your work is narrative-based, with every piece telling a story. How do you construct those narratives?

I think about this a lot, partly because of my own experience with language. Russian is my first language, English my second, and now I'm learning French here in Montréal. There have always been barriers, but as a visual artist, I can bypass all of them. My target audience is, in a sense, my grandmother in Poland. If she can understand the piece, I've done my job. Because

PHI
Old Montréal

Darling Foundry
Griffintown

Arsenal Contemporary Art
Griffintown

so much of my work is public, I want it to be inviting. I want it to make people rediscover something. The most exciting part of storytelling for me is surprise, hiding something in the work that rewards a second look. My large Mile End mural is about a hundred feet by a hundred feet, and the landmarks from the surrounding neighborhood are embedded within it. There's a large sun, and if you look closely, the typography around it references the neighborhood. There are Easter eggs inside the water tower, inside the barber shop. People come back to it, and each time they see something different.

Montréal has one of the most vibrant mural scenes in North America. Which neighborhoods do you think are essential?

Saint-Laurent is the place to start. It's the street that divides central Montréal, and as you walk up it, you're moving through over a decade of accumulated work by world-renowned artists. Every corner has been painted. Then there's the area around Mile End and Gaspé. It has the highest concentration of artists of anywhere I've been in Canada. Two blocks, and it's just creatives, studios, entrepreneurs, coffee shops, everyone meeting downstairs, ideas everywhere.

What are the art spaces and cultural venues you find essential in Montréal?

The *PHI* center is amazing. They bring together technology and art in a way that feels genuinely new. I also love the *Darling Foundry*, which always has strong shows. And then there's *Arsenal*, which is criminally underrated. They have one of the largest collections of contemporary art I've ever seen,

Montréal Museum of Fine Arts
Golden Square Mile

Satay Brothers
Saint-Henri

Mano Cornuto
Griffintown

Parc La Fontaine
Le Plateau-Mont-Royal

Le Majestique
Le Plateau-Mont-Royal

and they're always doing something new. *The Fine Arts Museum* is essential, too, and has put on some of my favorite exhibitions in recent years.

What are your favorite spots to eat in Montréal, places that feel like home?

Satay Brothers is fantastic. It's next to my studio, and I go there all the time. The vibe is electric, always overly crowded in the best way. It's Southeast Asian food, very modernized. And then there's *Mano Cornuto*, which everyone is talking about right now. It's a small Italian restaurant on a corner, nothing flashy, but the food is phenomenal. Even the prime minister has eaten there. If you want to know who's who in Montréal's creative scene, just go there for dinner.

If you want to experience Montréal by night, where do you go?

In summer, I always start at *Parc La Fontaine*. It's one of the central parks where the Mile End meets the Plateau, and it's where everyone gathers at the start of the evening. You can drink in the park, have a picnic and listen to musicians who just show up. That's where you collect all your people before the night begins. I also like to grab oysters and a drink at *Le Majestique* on Saint-Laurent, then take the bike down to the canal. Montréal by night in summer is something else entirely. There's always something happening: the *Jazz Festival*, *Piknic Électronik*, F1, the *MURAL Festival*. On any given night, there's a comedy festival or a concert or a block party. In winter, there's *Igloofest*, an outdoor electronic music festival at the Old

Café Olimpico
Mile End

Tommy's Cafe
Old Montréal

Notre-Dame Basilica of Montréal
Old Montréal

Atwater Market
Saint-Henri

Port. It's sometimes –25°C, but 10,000 people show up anyway. You're dancing outside in the cold, and it's one of the most alive things I've ever experienced.

How do you spend a day off in the city?

I'm a big coffee person, and I love working from coffee shops. I love the chaos, the sound of other people. *Café Olimpico* in Mile End is one of my favorites. A lot of my friends live in that neighborhood, so we often end up meeting there. I also love *Tommy's*, a coffee shop in the heart of Old Montréal. The layers of history are everywhere: the texture, the patterns. I go there to collect visual ideas. I pop into the *[Notre-Dame] Basilica* sometimes too, not for religious reasons, but to study the composition, the way the light falls, the patterns used in the art. I do a lot of biking. I like to ride down to the canal near the *Atwater Market*, which is close to my studio. It's one of the most beautiful bike paths in the city. In summer, Montréal basically lives outside.

Where do you go for a day trip when you need to get out of the city?

Bromont is fantastic. It's about an hour out of the city in the Eastern Townships, and it has this small-town quality that's hard to find: organic cheeses, hiking, fresh air, everyone a bit outdoorsy. But what's surprised me recently is the art scene that's been developing there. Galleries have been opening, and I keep seeing friends' work showing up in them. And if I have a bit more time, Quebec City feels like an entirely different world.

Sea Land

Think Big

In a former 19th-century shipyard on the Lachine Canal, *Arsenal Contemporary Art* is Canada's largest private art center. The building retains much of its original industrial structure, giving the space a raw scale that few galleries can match. The program is dedicated to Canadian contemporary art within a global context, with past solo shows by Anselm Kiefer, Donald Judd, Ugo Rondinone, Jon Rafman and Michel de Broin, whose 2017 *Thresholds* (photo) was made from reclaimed subway doors and motion detectors. An artist residency program runs year-round, bringing in creators from around the world.

• Arsenal Contemporary Art, 2020 William Street, Griffintown, arsenalcontemporary.com

Art & Design

From Concrete to Canvas

Montréal wears its creativity in concrete, glass and canvas. From a housing complex stacked like concrete boxes to the world's tallest inclined tower, discover the buildings, museums and galleries where the city's artistic vision comes to life.

The Heavyweight

Founded in 1860, the *Montréal Museum of Fine Arts* is the oldest art museum in Canada and one of the largest, with nearly 47,000 works spread across five interconnected pavilions. The holdings range from works by European old masters—including Rodin, Monet and Rembrandt—to pieces by Canadian and Indigenous artists, decorative arts and design objects, and collections spanning ancient civilizations and cultures from around the world. Its exhibition program consistently brings major international shows, like Richard Avedon and the Torlonia Collection of Roman sculpture, cementing its status as a cultural heavyweight.

• Montréal Museum of Fine Arts, 1380 Sherbrooke Street West, Golden Square Mile, mbam.qc.ca

Photos: Jaysson Gallant/Tourisme Montréal, Eva Blue/Tourisme Montréal, Studio Lux

Memory Lane

The city's most important social history museum, the *McCord Stewart* traces the city's past through 2.5 million images, objects, documents and works of art accumulated since its founding in 1921. Its standout holding is the UNESCO-inscribed Notman Photographic Archives. The collection comprises 200,000 glass-plate negatives from a Victorian-era Montréal studio that document the city's social fabric for nearly eight decades. The exhibition program is ambitious, ranging from fashion and Indigenous cultures to long-term documentary commissions that put local photographers in direct dialogue with the changing neighborhoods.

• McCord Stewart Museum, 690 Sherbrooke Street West, McGill, musee-mccord-stewart.ca

The Big Tilt

Designed by French architect Roger Taillibert for the 1976 Montréal Olympics, the *Montréal Tower* is the world's tallest inclined tower, rising 541 feet at a 45-degree angle. It wasn't completed until 1987 and sat largely vacant for decades. In 2018, Provencher_Roy replaced its concrete cladding with a glass curtain wall, revealing the dramatic angled columns for the first time. A funicular carries visitors to the summit for panoramic views stretching to the Laurentian Mountains. Closed for renovations until at least spring 2027, the tower is scheduled to reopen with rooftop access and a new glass-enclosed funicular.

• Montréal Tower, 4141 Pierre-De Coubertin Avenue, Hochelaga-Maisonneuve, parcolympique.qc.ca

Photo: Elias Touil

Ice to Innovation

Completed in 2016 by MSDL Architectes, the student center of *École de technologie supérieure* takes its form from an icehouse that once stood on the site. The crystal-like volume rises in angular facets of glass and steel, its appearance shifting as the light changes throughout the day. Carved-out sections on its south and east sides open onto a park extending into the atrium. Inside, a cantilevered steel truss echoes the railway bridges and industrial structures of the neighborhood, while the atrium ceiling is finished in cherrywood panels.

• Maison des Étudiants de l'ÉTS, 1220 Notre-Dame Street West, Griffintown, etsmtl.ca

Concrete Dreams

What started as a student thesis became one of the most ambitious housing experiments of the 20th century. Designed by Moshe Safdie for Expo 67, *Habitat 67* lines the St. Lawrence River with 354 prefabricated concrete modules stacked in irregular geometric formations. Each unit steps back from the one below, giving every apartment a private rooftop garden, natural light and unobstructed views of the river. External walkways and terraces connect the units into a vertical street network, creating something between a hillside village and a futurist megastructure. Tours are available.

• Habitat 67, 2600 Pierre-Dupuy Avenue, Cité-du-Havre, habitat67.com

Photos: Eva Blue/Tourisme Montréal, Stéphane Brügger/Tourisme Montréal

A Photo Showcase

Wild in the Streets

Chantal Levesque

Before turning her lens on animals, Chantal Levesque spent years photographing concerts and protests and playing guitar in an all-female death-metal band. Since 2015, she has channeled that same eye for energy and unpredictability into pet photography, developing a cinematic, moody aesthetic that sets her work apart. Her photobook *Bark and Roll: Icôns & Rebelles* raised money for animal rescues and shelters with rock-star-inspired portraits of local dogs, while *Chasing Shadows* is an ongoing project dedicated to photographing adopted black animals.

You spent years shooting concerts and events before pivoting to pet photography. What drove that shift, and how do the earlier influences shape the way you approach animals as subjects?

The pivot came down to making a living. Concert and event photography doesn't pay much. Most of the time, you get a press pass in exchange for the photos, and that's it. I wanted photography to be my career, but I also needed it to be something I loved. I love animals, and I saw a real connection between the energy of concerts and working with them. Animals are unpredictable. They have huge personalities, and you have to observe and capture the right moment, which is exactly what I did in concert photography. I've always loved the chaos and unpredictability of concerts, the moving lights, the energy, and I found all of that in dog photography. It let me keep doing what I love while actually making a living from it.

You describe your goal as capturing each animal's individual personality rather than a generic cute portrait. How do you work with animals to get beyond that?

I start by talking to the owners. I have a questionnaire to get to know the animal before we even start: Are they shy or outgoing? Energetic or zen? That gives me a sense of what I want to capture going in. But I'm also very open to what the dog gives me on the day. If the owner tells me their dog is calm and quiet, and the dog goes completely nuts, I'll capture that too. I try not to force anything. I observe, I learn their patterns and behaviors, and I let things happen naturally. I've also picked up enough knowledge about dog behavior from trainers over the years to recognize what I'm seeing and know when to press the shutter.

Your images have a cinematic quality that sets them apart from typical pet photography. How did you develop that visual language?

I love movies. It's my main pastime, and I watch a lot of them, at least 10 or 15 a month, mostly older, obscure, weird, independent stuff. Moody things. And I think what you consume inevitably shows in what you create. My sensibilities come through in what I see and what I choose to capture. I've absorbed so much of that visual language that it's just become part of how I see.

Your Chasing Shadows *project was born from a personal love of black animals and the discovery that they're the last to be adopted in shelters. How did that personal connection become a long-term photographic project?*

As a creative, I really wanted a personal project, something I shoot for myself rather than for clients. I had a black dog as a kid and a black cat as a young adult—my first pet of my own, named Diablo. And when I started working with shelters, the volunteers told me that black animals are consistently the last to be adopted. I even hear from owners of black dogs that people will sometimes cross the street to avoid walking past them. For me, the project became a way to show them as the beautiful, sweet, extraordinary animals they are. I just wanted people to see them as the rock stars they really are.

You shoot both dogs and cats. How different are they to work with?

Very different. Dogs are generally more trainable, and you can take them outside, which opens up a lot of options. Cats are mostly indoors, in their own environment, and you have to be much more patient and observant with them. You study their patterns, notice where they like to go. Cats are visually curious, so if you move something, they'll investigate it. Want a cat by a window? Put a chair there and wait. Dogs respond more to sounds and smells. I use squeaky toys and duck calls, the kind hunters use to attract wild animals, to get dogs to perk up and look in the right direction. Cats observe. Dogs want to please. Once you understand that distinction, you can work with both on their own terms.

MARCHÉ

Picture This

Don't let the "comic book publisher" label fool you. *Drawn & Quarterly* is one of Montréal's great cultural institutions and one of the world's most respected graphic novel publishers. Shelves are packed with beautifully illustrated books, literary comics, art titles and works by celebrated international cartoonists, alongside a carefully curated selection of fiction and nonfiction. Regular author talks, book launches and exhibitions have made it a cornerstone of the local creative community. Even if graphic novels aren't usually your thing, this is the sort of place that can change your mind.

• Drawn & Quarterly, 176 Bernard Street West, Mile End, drawnandquarterly.com

Shops

The Local Hunt

From vintage boutiques and homegrown streetwear to famous public markets, the city rewards those who love the thrill of the hunt. Come curious. You never know what you'll take home.

Beautiful Chaos

Eva B is often the first thrift store people visit after arriving in Montréal. The derelict-looking, graffiti-covered exterior, plastered with an old *Rocky Horror Picture Show* poster and years of local flyers, hints at what's inside. Expect a chaotic mix of art, fashion and vintage mannequins, with platform shoes, dolls and records hanging from the ceiling. The main floor holds classic vintage pieces, while the upstairs offers affordable modern secondhand finds. Prices stay reasonable throughout, and the on-site café is famous for its samosas and one-dollar espressos.

• Eva B, 2015 Boulevard St-Laurent, Quartier des Spectacles, boutiqueevab.com

Decked Out

What began as a Montréal skate crew has grown into one of Canada's most influential streetwear labels. *Dime*'s flagship store reflects the brand's understated aesthetic, stocking its sought-after collections of graphic tees, denim, outerwear and accessories alongside carefully selected collaborations and limited releases. Rooted in skate culture but embraced far beyond it, the brand has built an international following while remaining proudly tied to its hometown. Even if you're not planning to buy anything, it's worth stopping by to get a feel for one of Montréal's biggest streetwear success stories.

• Dime, 3632 Saint-Laurent Boulevard, Plateau Mont-Royal, dimemtl.com

Vintage Revival

Part vintage store, part community hub, *Marché Floh* has become a go-to address for the city's Gen Z fashion crowd. The curated boutique champions vintage, upcycled and independent labels, with racks that mix Y2K staples, streetwear and one-off finds rather than fast fashion. Regular pop-ups, creative collaborations and in-store events keep the space feeling fresh, while the ever-changing inventory means no two visits are quite the same. Come with an open mind and a little patience, and you're likely to leave with something nobody else is wearing.

• Marché Floh, two locations, marchefloh.com

Photo: dezieff/Jeff Frenette

Market Value

No visit to Montréal is complete without wandering through *Jean-Talon Market,* one of North America's largest public markets. Year-round, local farmers, cheesemakers, bakers and specialty food vendors gather beneath colorful awnings, creating a place where you can easily lose an afternoon. Arrive hungry and graze your way through Québec cheeses, fresh produce, maple treats and seasonal delicacies before filling a tote bag with picnic supplies. The jam-filled pączki from *Pâtisserie Wawel* are a must, as are the generously stuffed lobster rolls from *Délices de la Mer,* the fresh seafood market you'll spot as soon as you enter.

• Jean-Talon Market, 7070 Henri-Julien Avenue, Little Italy, marchespublics-mtl.com

Photos: Dominique Viau, Maxwell Neubacher

Riverside Harvest

Housed in a beautiful Art Deco building along the Lachine Canal, *Atwater Market* has been feeding Montréalers since 1933. While its butchers, fishmongers and produce stalls are the first thing you'll notice, it's equally worth visiting for the specialty shops, bakeries and cafés that surround the market. Grab lunch, then stroll the canal with fresh bread, local cheese and a bottle of cider in tow. In the warmer months, it's one of the city's favorite picnic destinations and the perfect excuse to spend an afternoon by the water.

• Atwater Market, 138 Atwater Avenue, Saint-Henri, marchespublics-mtl.com

Hugo Lavictoire

The City Flows Through It

For three decades, Hugo Lavictoire has been encouraging Montréalers to look at the St. Lawrence a little differently. The founder of KSF and later Rafting Montréal helped put urban river surfing and paddlesports on the map, turning a stretch of the Lachine Rapids into one of the city's most unexpected playgrounds. He's the perfect person to discuss misconceptions about the river, the city's evolving relationship with its waterfront and why September might just be the city's best-kept secret.

You've spent more than 30 years introducing people to the St. Lawrence. What's the biggest misconception people have about the river?

People still think it's dirty, polluted or even dangerous. That's probably the biggest misconception. One of our goals has always been to change that. Every day we take people onto the water, and they come back saying, "I had no idea this existed." They're surprised by how clean the river is, how beautiful it is and how accessible it can be. If people leave with a different relationship to the river and a greater respect for it, then we've done our job.

For decades, you've been on the river for most of the year. Do you have a favorite season?

That's a difficult question because I'm out there for nine months of the year, so every season has something special. But if I had to choose, I'd say September. The water is still warm, the crowds begin to thin out, and the conditions are often fantastic. That said, from May through September is really the sweet spot if you're visiting Montréal and want to experience the river.

You helped pioneer river surfing and urban paddling long before they became mainstream. Was there a moment when you realized Montréal was finally starting to see the river differently?

Yes, but it happened much later than people think. In the beginning, we were just seen as a bunch of surf guys and kayak bums. Around 2015, things really started to change. The city invested in infrastructure around the surf wave we teach on, building proper access, changing rooms and facilities because they recognized people wanted to be there. Families even started moving into the neighborhood to be closer to the river. That was the moment I realized Montréal had started embracing the water again.

What has the St. Lawrence taught you that the city itself can't?

Respect. Respect for nature, for water quality and for the sheer power of the river. The St. Lawrence isn't an ordinary river. The current is incredibly strong, the waves are powerful and you have to earn your way into

Photos: Mike Hitelman, Guy François Haché

Le Café Magda
LaSalle

Café Après Soleil
Verdun

Atwater Market
Saint-Henri

Satay Brothers
Saint-Henri

it. You can't rush that process. Every time someone overcomes their fear and catches a wave—or even just steps into the river for the first time—it's a real accomplishment.

What's the best way for someone to experience the river for the first time?

Rafting is probably the easiest and most exciting introduction. It's suitable for almost everyone, from families to groups of friends, and you experience the rapids from right inside them while learning about Montréal's history, the First Nations who lived here and the river itself. We always joke it's for people aged 7 to 77. It's safe, it's exciting and it gives you a completely different perspective on the city.

If you wanted someone visiting Montréal to fall in love with the city in a single afternoon, where would you send them?

If they're coming to us, I'd tell them to spend time in the southwest. Grab a coffee or sandwich at *Le Café Magda*, have lunch at *Après Soleil* with the surfers, then explore the river. Later, head towards *Atwater Market* and finish with dinner at *Satay Brothers*. It shows a side of Montréal that many visitors never discover.

What's your favorite neighborhood in Montréal?

If you love nature, I think this part of the city [where we are located in LaSalle] is hard to beat. You're on the islands, surrounded by water, and it almost feels like being by the ocean. If you're looking for cafés, restaurants and shopping, I'd send you to Plateau Mont-Royal or Villeray. They both have a great local energy.

What's kept you excited after all these years?

No two days are ever the same. One morning I might be teaching seven-year-olds how to paddle. In the afternoon, I'm guiding a bachelor party through the rapids. The next day I'm leading a surf lesson, teaching kayak instructors or

working in the surf shop. We started with kayaking, added river surfing, then paddleboarding, and eventually rafting. I never really had the chance to get bored.

What's the best way to experience Montréal?

By bike, without a doubt. The BIXI bike-share system makes it incredibly easy to explore, and you can combine it with the Metro whenever you want to cover longer distances. Montréal is a big city, but it's one that rewards slowing down and discovering neighborhoods at street level.

Why should people visit Montréal?

It's unlike anywhere else in North America. We're this French-speaking island surrounded by English-speaking Canada and the US, with influences from all over the world. You have historic architecture, modern neighborhoods and, at the same time, incredible nature right on the city's doorstep. More than anything, I'd encourage visitors to be curious. Learn a few words of French, venture beyond the obvious tourist sights, and don't forget that Montréal is an island. The river is part of its identity. You just have to go out and discover it.

Outdoors

Urban Wild

Montréal's wild side is closer than you think. From river surfing and whitewater rapids to sandy beaches and mountain trails, discover the places where the city lets nature take over.

Where Legends Roll

More than just a skatepark, *Peace Park* is widely considered the birthplace of Montréal's modern street-skating scene. Beneath the overpass near the Palais des congrès, its granite ledges, stairs and open plaza have drawn generations of skateboarders since the 1990s, serving as a proving ground for local talent and a pilgrimage site for skaters from around the world. Even if you're not riding, it's worth stopping by to watch the constant flow of tricks, soak up the energy and experience a living piece of skateboarding history.

- Peace Park, 1197 Saint-Dominique Street, Quartier des Spectacles, peacepark.com

Peak Montréal

One of the city's most iconic destinations, *Mount Royal Park* is beloved by visitors and locals alike for its skyline views and wooded trails. Early risers hike up to catch the sunrise, while others make the night-time climb for a glittering view of the city lights and the chance to spot the park's surprisingly tame raccoons. Whether you walk, bike, drive or take the bus to the top, the mountain is at its most spectacular in autumn, when the surrounding trees explode in brilliant shades of red, orange and gold.

- Mount Royal Park, 1260 Remembrance Road, Mount Royal

Photos: Mural Untitled by OSGEMEOS/Kenan Aboshi/Tourisme Montréal, Tony Webster CC BY-SA 4.0, Eva Blue/Tourisme Montréal

Flow State

The Lachine Canal blends the city's industrial past and its greener present, running from the Old Port to the borough of Lachine. It's an easy place to spend an afternoon, whether you're picnicking on the grass with provisions from nearby *Atwater Market* or exploring the water by kayak, canoe or giant swan-shaped paddle boat. Bike rentals make it just as easy to follow the towpath on two wheels. In winter, a well-maintained snowshoe trail winds past historic buildings, trees and pockets of wildlife, offering a quieter glimpse into the city's past.

• Lachine Canal, various neighborhoods

Photo: Artem Onoprienko

Park Yourself

Perhaps the most romantic park in the city, *Parc La Fontaine* remains one of the most beloved green spaces in Montréal. Old trees, bocce courts, live music and a central fountain draw crowds for activities, biking, strolling or simply stretching out in the grass. Nature lovers should keep an eye out for the park's rare blond squirrels and listen for the European starling, a bird known for mimicking other songbirds. For the best views and maximum atmosphere, plan to stay until golden hour, roughly an hour before sunset.

• Parc La Fontaine, Plateau-Mont-Royal

Flower Power

In the middle of the St. Lawrence River, *Parc Jean-Drapeau* is home to three permanent mosaïculture sculptures of extraordinary scale. Each is built from hundreds of thousands of living plants woven onto metal frameworks and arranged by color, texture and shape. *Mother Earth* rises 36 feet above the *Jardins des Floralies*, while *The Man Who Planted Trees* pays tribute to Frédéric Back's Oscar-winning film. Six YY figures, inspired by the park's Expo 67 logo, are scattered across both islands. The works evolve with the seasons and are at their most vivid from June through September.

• Jardins des Floralies and Mosaïcultures, Parc Jean-Drapeau, Île Notre-Dame, parcjeandrapeau.com

Photos: Bertrand Exertier/Tourisme Montréal, meunierd / Shutterstock.com

The People's Beach

Opened in 2019, Verdun Beach quickly became one of the city's favorite places to escape the summer heat. The St. Lawrence has a reputation for rough waters, but lifeguards and daily water-quality testing make this a safe place to take the plunge. The setup is simple: sand, a grassy hill, river views and room to spread out, with a climbing wall and waterslide to keep kids busy. But the real attraction is the scene. On a sunny afternoon, Verdun Beach becomes a cross-section of the neighborhood, with everyone looking for a little riverside action.

• Verdun Beach, 4110 Boulevard LaSalle, Verdun

Common Ground

Where the city meets nature, *Jeanne-Mance Park* stretches along the foot of Mount Royal and serves as a year-round gathering place for the surrounding neighborhoods. In warm weather, locals spread out for picnics, yoga, tennis and pickup volleyball, while kids make a beeline for the playground. When winter arrives, the park shifts into cross-country skiing, tobogganing and ice skating. Festivals and concerts fill its calendar year-round. It's a fitting expression of the city's love of community and outdoor living, drawing locals outdoors in every season.

• Jeanne-Mance Park, Plateau Mont-Royal

The Endless Ride

Think you need an ocean to surf? Think again. Montréal has quietly become one of North America's top river-surfing destinations, thanks to the standing waves of the St. Lawrence River. Unlike ocean breaks, these stationary waves let surfers ride continuously for minutes without paddling back out. The city's best-known break, Habitat 67, sits beside the iconic housing complex of the same name. For a more forgiving wave, head to Vague à Guy, another favorite among the local surf community. Together, these spots are a perfect reminder that Montréal doesn't need a coastline to make waves.

• St. Lawrence River

Photos: Saute-Moutons/Tourisme Montréal, Mike Hitelman

Wild Waters

For adventure seekers, the Lachine Rapids offer excellent access to nature close to downtown. Local outfitters rent equipment and offer lessons in paddleboarding, rafting, kayaking and even river surfing. Beginners should stick to guided instruction, as the rapids are no joke. Parks, benches, lounge chairs and art installations along the river offer quieter ways to take in the scenery. It's a rare Montréal experience: a wild stretch of the St. Lawrence where you can paddle, surf or simply sit back and enjoy nature. You escape the city without ever actually leaving it.

• Lachine Rapids, 7770 Boulevard LaSalle, LaSalle

N10.AS
TEE PEE

Meyer Billurcu

Always Listening

Meyer Billurcu first noticed touring bands skipping Montréal in the early 2000s. Rather than complain about it, he started booking them himself. What began as two friends hosting a radio show at Concordia University's CJLO soon became Blue Skies Turn Black, the independent concert promotion company that Billurcu has spent decades building into a leading force in live music. Along the way, he helped launch *Il Motore*, the music venue that would eventually become *Bar Le Ritz PDB*, while championing emerging artists and helping shape Montréal's independent music community. Yet ask him what keeps him motivated after thousands of shows, and the answer has little to do with the business itself: It's his genuine love of music and the constant thrill of discovering something new.

You've spent more than two decades booking shows in Montréal. What keeps you inspired by the city?

Honestly, it's the crowds. Montréal has some of the best audiences in the world. I've been to a lot of shows in a lot of different cities, and people just don't seem as excited as they are here. There's something really infectious about seeing a room full of people completely locked into the music. I still go to shows all the time, whether it's one we're promoting or somebody else's. I still get excited when I hear a band I've never listened to before. That feeling never really goes away. Montréal just breeds creativity, and that's why I'm still here.

What makes Montréal different from every other city?

I've always thought of Montréal as a "small big city." You get everything you'd want from a major city, but without feeling like you're constantly rushing somewhere. There's a laid-back rhythm here that you don't find in places like Toronto. You can spend the day walking between neighborhoods, grabbing a coffee, digging through record stores, running into friends and finishing the night at a show. It never feels forced.

The music community has changed dramatically since Blue Skies Turn Black began. What stands out to you?

The scene is always changing. When people look back at Montréal around 2005, they usually talk about Arcade Fire, Wolf Parade and that whole explosion, but affordable rent was a huge part of that story. Artists could actually afford to move here and make art. That's changed over the last 20 years, but what's exciting now is seeing younger artists and promoters create their own spaces instead of relying on traditional venues. Some of the most interesting things happening in Montréal aren't happening inside established clubs anymore. They're happening in DIY spaces. Every generation builds its own scene.

Photo: Doug Hollingworth

Bar Le Ritz PDB
Mile-Ex

Bagel Etc
Le Plateau-Mont-Royal

Cheap Thrills
Downtown

Phonopolis
Mile End

Iconoglace
Quartier des Spectacles

Casa del Popolo
Mile End

La Sala Rossa
Le Plateau-Mont-Royal

If someone only had 48 hours in Montréal, how would you tell them to spend it?

I'd start with brunch at *Bagel Etc.* Then I'd spend the afternoon wandering through the Plateau and Mile End. Go thrifting. Browse a few record stores. Grab a coffee. Montréal is one of those cities where the best plan is not really having one. I'd probably stop in *Cheap Thrills* or *Phonopolis*, maybe pick up a six-pack and spend some time in Jeanne-Mance or Jarry Park before heading for dinner. Then I'd finish the night exactly how I usually do: with a show. That's a pretty perfect Montréal day.

Where do you send visiting musicians when they ask what to do before soundcheck?

Iconoglace [ice cream]. It's one of those little places that just feels very Montréal to me. Everything is made in-house, and they offer vegan and gluten-free options for everything.

Which neighborhood best represents Montréal right now?

For someone visiting the city, I'd still say the Plateau and Mile End. That's where so much of Montréal's independent music culture still lives. You've got *Casa del Popolo, La Sala Rossa, L'Escogriffe*, incredible cafés, record stores, bars. You could spend an entire weekend there without running out of things to do.

Where are you grabbing coffee?

Le Moineau Masqué. It's close to Mont-Royal Metro but just tucked away enough that it still feels like a real neighborhood café.

Where are you heading for lunch?

Ohayo Café. Everything on the menu is great, but I always end up getting the ramen. Best in the city if you ask me.

L'Escogriffe
Le Plateau-Mont-Royal

Le Moineau Masqué
Le Plateau-Mont-Royal

Ohayo Café
Le Plateau-Mont-Royal

Petit Alep
Villeray

La Cité
Milton-Park

Drawn & Quarterly
Mile End

St-Viateur Bagel
Mile End

B Bagel
Pointe-Saint-Charles

Greenspot
Saint-Henri

Rialto Theatre
Mile End

La Binerie Mont-Royal
Plateau-Mont-Royal

Dinner after a successful show?

Petit Alep. It's one of my favorite restaurants in Montréal. Amazing Middle Eastern food, great cocktails and a really relaxed atmosphere. It's the kind of place that feels like a celebration without trying too hard.

Which venue best captures Montréal's music scene?

Casa del Popolo. It's basically a rite of passage for local bands. At some point every Montréal band should play Casa. It feels like one of the cultural anchors of the city's music community.

What should visitors have on their headphones while exploring Montréal?

That answer changes every day. Today, I'd say *Face Control* by Handsome Furs. Dan Boeckner [of Wolf Parade] has made so much incredible music, and that's still one of my favorites.

Where do you go when you need a break from work?

The rooftop pool at *La Cité*. It's one of those places that people don't always know about. You can spend an afternoon there and completely forget you're in the middle of the city.

Favorite record store?

That's like asking someone to choose their favorite child. If I can only pick one, I'll say Cheap Thrills. I've been shopping there forever and have a great relationship with the staff. Sorry to all my other children.

Favorite bookstore?

Drawn & Quarterly. Whether you're into graphic novels, art books or literature, you'll find something there. I've been going for years, and I never leave empty-handed.

If you weren't putting on concerts, what do you think you'd be doing?

Probably wishing I was. But honestly, I'd love to own a café and record store where all my friends could hang out. That sounds like a pretty good life.

Finish this sentence: You haven't really experienced Montréal until…

…you've stayed out all night and watched the sun come up in the middle of summer.

Best bagel?

St-Viateur Bagel is still the GOAT. But if you're looking for something closer to a New York–style bagel, *B Bagel* is fantastic.

Best poutine?

Greenspot, an old-school diner in St-Henri that also serves burgers and hot dogs.

Favorite festival?

Taverne Tour. I love club festivals more than big outdoor festivals. The energy is wild.

Favorite walk?

Along the Lachine Canal. You can walk all the way from the Old Port to Lachine.

Best place to catch the sunset?

The Rialto [Theatre] rooftop, if you know how to get up there.

A hidden gem you almost don't want to share?

La Binerie [Mont-Royal] on Saint-Denis. One of the best breakfasts in the city, and it's been around since 1938.

One thing visitors always get wrong about Montréal?

That there's an underground city. There isn't. It's a myth.

Electronic Dreams

Founded in Montréal in 2000, *MUTEK* has become one of the world's most respected festivals for electronic music and digital art. Held every August, it unfolds over six nights with live electronic music, real-time audiovisual performances, installations and immersive experiences staged across concert halls, outdoor venues and unconventional spaces. The program consistently favors experimentation and risk, spotlighting artists who blur the boundaries between sound, image and technology. Its influence now extends far beyond Montréal, with satellite editions in Mexico City, Tokyo, Barcelona, Buenos Aires and beyond.

• MUTEK, Quartier des Spectacles, mutek.org

Gather

City in Motion

From all-night art marathons and major music festivals to roving raves and Sunday drum circles, these are the events that bring the city together.

Circus City

Montréal Complètement Cirque offers one of the most accessible ways to experience the city's world-class circus culture. Acrobats, aerialists, trapeze artists and clowns take over everything from street corners to formal stages for 11 days each summer. While many festival venues cluster around Place des Arts, the action spreads across boroughs throughout the city. A mix of ticketed and free performances bridges English- and French-language programming, making it an easy pick for families and thrill-seekers of every age looking for something genuinely awe-inspiring.

• Montréal Complètement Cirque, various locations, montrealcompletementcirque.com

Photos: Daphné Caron/Tourisme Montréal, Trung Dung Nguyen, Eva Blue/Tourisme Montréa

Mic Drop

Launched in the 1980s, *Just for Laughs* has grown into one of Canada's biggest cultural exports, with festivals now held around the world. Montréal's original event remains the largest comedy festival anywhere, spread across multiple downtown venues, with Quartier des Spectacles at its heart. The lineup mixes rising talent with major stars—think Mae Martin, Jimmy Fallon and David Letterman—and formats range from standup and sketch to improv and curated galas. Most headline shows require tickets, but many outdoor performances throughout downtown are free.

• Just for Laughs, various locations, montreal.hahaha.com

Dance Without Borders

For two weeks in late May and early June, *Festival TransAmériques* (FTA) brings a jolt of electricity to the vibrant theater and dance scenes. A curated slate of local and international productions takes over the city's stages, with recent editions featuring work from countries like South Africa, Switzerland, Argentina and Kyrgyzstan. Each production comes with English and French captions as needed. For shows that are lower cost and even more avant-garde, the smaller OFFTA festival runs simultaneously. Either way, the atmosphere will be buzzing and the auditoriums packed.

• Festival TransAmériques, Quartier des Spectacles, fta.ca

Photos: Eric Myre, Trung Dung Nguyen

The Gallery Below

Every spring, *Art Souterrain* takes over Montréal's RÉSO—the vast underground pedestrian network connecting metro stations, office towers and cultural venues beneath downtown—into a two-week contemporary art circuit. Installations, video works, sound pieces and performances by local and international artists are embedded across miles of underground corridors and connected buildings, turning the city's underworld into an unlikely gallery. Organized around a central theme, each edition is curated as a single immersive route that rewards both deliberate exploration and accidental discovery.

• Art Souterrain, RÉSO Underground City, Downtown, artsouterrain.com

Photos: Samuel Boisvert, Eva Blue/Tourisme Montréal

Up All Night

Nuit Blanche brings experimental art into the heart of the city for an all-night celebration. While the arts festival takes place around the world, Montréal's version is unusual for unfolding in the depths of February. The cold is part of the fun. Expect immersive installations, all-night improv, outdoor performances and even a Ferris wheel spinning through the winter darkness. Artists take over venues across the city until sunrise. Part of the *Montréal en Lumière* festival, Nuit Blanche embodies the city's refusal to let winter get in the way of a good time.

• Nuit Blanche, Quartier des Spectacles and various locations, nuitblanchemtl.com

Bass Island

Every August, Parc Jean-Drapeau transforms into one of Canada's premier electronic music playgrounds for *ÎLESONIQ*. This massive two-day festival unites global headliners, rising DJs and thousands of dance music faithful for house, techno and bass-heavy sounds. It's one of the city's most colorful gatherings and proof that the city knows how to throw a party. Set on an island across the St. Lawrence River, the festival feels worlds away from the city, with massive stage productions, waterfront sunsets, surprise collabs and an energy that doesn't let up until the final beat drops.

- ÎLESONIQ, Parc Jean-Drapeau, Île Sainte-Hélène, ilesoniq.com

Party in the Ice Age

Why wait for summer to dance until sunrise? When the temperatures drop, *Igloofest* turns the Old Port into a neon-lit playground where thousands brave the winter temps for DJs, dancing and epic outdoor production. The cold is part of the appeal: Bundled-up crowds turn the waterfront into a sea of vintage snowsuits where loud, bright and tacky is the style of choice. Spread across four weekends, the "coldest music festival in the world" adds fire pits, food trucks and hot drinks to the mix, while VIP tickets include access to a heated terrace.

- Igloofest, Old Port of Montréal, igloofest.ca

Photos: Eva Blue/Tourisme Montréal, Danh & Nico/Tourisme Montréal

Circle of Sound

Les Tam-Tams captures Montréal's bohemian, free-spirited energy better than almost anywhere else in the city. Every Sunday from May through September, drummers, dancers, artisans and spectators gather near the Sir George-Étienne Cartier Monument in Jeanne-Mance Park to celebrate life and community. A wide circle forms as drummers of every skill level jam together on *djembes* and bongos, while dancers move to the collective rhythm and onlookers relax on the grass. The vibe is entirely come-as-you-are, making it a natural gathering place for some of the city's most unconventional characters.

• Les Tam-Tams, 4200 Avenue du Parc, Plateau Mont-Royal

Sunday Sessions

Piknic Électronik is a beloved outdoor music festival, taking over Île Sainte-Hélène every Sunday from May through September. Dazzling projections, food trucks and a rotating lineup of local and international DJs draw a loyal crowd, many of whom buy season passes rather than single tickets. Expect wild outfits, quirky dance moves and set lists that seem to awaken the soul. Lifelong ravers and curious newcomers are equally welcome, creating a scene where the energy is contagious and boredom simply isn't an option.

• Piknic Électronik, Jardin Le Petit Prince, Parc Jean-Drapeau, 1 Circuit Gilles-Villeneuve, piknicelectronik.com

Photos: Eva Blue/Tourisme Montréal, Canadian Tourism Commission

Blue Notes

No summer is complete without the *Montréal Jazz Festival*, which has hosted global stars like Stevie Wonder, Paul Simon and Diana Krall over the years. Best of all, most shows are free. Locals and travelers fill the streets each evening to catch concerts across three festival stages, or head to Place des Arts for a ticketed headliner. All-ages programming draws people from every background to dance and listen together. More than any other event, the nonprofit Jazz Festival embodies Montréal's love for accessible art, and it's worth planning a trip around.

- Montréal Jazz Festival, Quartier des Spectacles, Ville-Marie, montrealjazzfest.com

Off the Grid

Founded in 2014, *OCTOV* has grown from a local techno collective into one of Montréal's most respected underground electronic music operations. Events move across industrial spaces, warehouses and unconventional venues, with locations rarely announced far in advance. Light design and video are central to the experience, with resident DJs and international bookings joined by VJs creating live visual counterparts to the music. Safety, inclusivity and community are taken seriously, shaping both the crowd and the atmosphere. Keep an eye on the schedule. Half the appeal is never quite knowing where the next party will be.

- OCTOV, various locations, octov.ca

Outdoor Sounds

Montréal is awash in summer festivals, and *Osheaga* is one of the biggest and best. The three-day, all-ages event takes over the same islands that hosted Expo 67, drawing around 140,000 people for a weekend of more than a hundred bands, multiple outdoor stages, local art and food vendors. Recent editions have featured big-name acts like the xx, Geese and Lorde. Despite the crowds, it's a chill introduction into how much the city loves being outside in summer and, of course, reveling in the music.

• Osheaga Music and Arts Festival, 1, circuit Gilles-Villeneuve, St. Helen's Island, osheaga.com

Paint the Town

Every June since 2013, *MURAL* has taken over Boulevard Saint-Laurent for 10 days, transforming Montréal's iconic Main into an open-air gallery. Local and international artists paint large-scale works live on walls, vehicles and temporary surfaces, while free concerts, block parties, food trucks and guided tours animate the boulevard. Founded on the belief that art belongs in public space and should be free for everyone, the festival has produced several dozen murals—including Shepard Fairey's *Mural Paix et Justice* (pictured)—since its inaugural edition.

• MURAL Festival, Saint-Laurent Boulevard, Plateau-Mont-Royal, muralfestival.com

Photos: Eva Blue/Tourisme Montréal

Music First

A fixture of Montréal's nightlife since the late 1990s, *Stereo* has earned an international reputation for marathon DJ sets and one of the world's most respected sound systems. Open from midnight onward on Friday and Saturday nights, it runs on a simple premise: no alcohol upstairs, no cameras, no distractions. Just house and techno channeled through a sound system built into three-foot-thick walls, over a sprung dance floor designed to absorb fatigue. If you're after bottle service and selfies, look elsewhere: Stereo is all about losing yourself in the music.

• Stereo, 858 Sainte-Catherine Street East, The Village, @stereoMontréal

Old-School Block Party

Founded in 1996 by local graffiti writers Seaz and Flow, *Under Pressure* is the oldest urban culture festival still active in North America. It's been run entirely by volunteers for nearly three decades. Every August, it takes over Sainte-Catherine Street East near Foufounes Électriques for a free two-day block party. Graffiti writers paint more than a hundred walls and vehicles, while DJs, MCs, breakdancers and skaters fill the surrounding streets. The spirit is deliberately grassroots, grounded in the same community-first ethos that sparked New York's block party culture in the 1970s.

• Under Pressure, Sainte-Catherine Street East, Quartier Latin, underpressure.ca

Keep on Truckin'

On the first Friday of each month from May to October, the Olympic Park Esplanade hosts one of the city's biggest open-air food festivals. More than 40 food trucks serve everything from Québec comfort food and gourmet burgers to tacos, dumplings and global street-food favorites. Live DJs, family-friendly activities and communal picnic tables give the event a neighborhood feel, while rotating themes and vendors keep each edition fresh. Arrive hungry, grab a few dishes to share and sample your way across Montréal's diverse food scene in a single evening.

• First Fridays, 4141 Pierre-de Coubertin Avenue, Mercier-Hochelaga-Maisonneuve, lespremiersvendredis.ca

Photos: Alison Slattery/Tourisme Montréal, Under Pressure

Get lost in the right places
OPEN
Off the map, but in your feed. Follow for hard-to-find recommendations.

Wellness

Take the Plunge

From floating spas on the St. Lawrence to tranquil Nordic retreats, these are the places to recharge and reset.

Photo: K Bialous/Destination Canada

Aqua Therapy

Forget that HIIT circuit for wellness; try a water circuit instead. That's the move at *Bota Bota*, a spa on a ship docked in the Old Port. In Japanese, the words *bota bota* represent the sound of a drop of water falling, and there's plenty of water on the refurbished ferry. Spa-goers move from dry sauna to cold plunge to relaxation and are never far from a St. Lawrence River view. Massages and water-themed facials aren't the only things on the menu: Stay a while for wine, beer and cocktails inside the on-site restaurant.

• Bota Bota, spa-sur-l'eau, 730 Mill Street, Old Port of Montréal, botabota.ca

Hot 'n' Cold

There's no time limit on the Scandinavian-style thermal journey here, a move between hot and cold with rests in between. There's also no Wi-Fi or talking. Amenities like a dry sauna, a hydrojet bath with a thermal waterfall, a cold pool, fresh juice service and a steam bath with eucalyptus help strip away urban cares, and massages are available either on their own or as part of the thermal experience. The centrally located spa is within walking distance of hotels, restaurants and attractions, including the *Notre-Dame Basilica*.

• Scandinave Spa Vieux-Montréal, 71 De la Commune Street West, Old Montréal, scandinave.com/vieux-montreal

Nordic Calm

This award-winning spa is tucked away on lush Nun's Island, an oasis of calm across from the southwest Verdun neighborhood. The Nordic-inspired journey starts with a choice of hot whirlpool, sauna or steam bath, then progresses to a cold Nordic bath and waterfall, followed by a respite with views of the water and nature. There's no limit to a stay, and add-on massages and spa treatments enhance the experience. The experience continues at Nord restaurant, which serves spa-appropriate flower-adorned plates and pretty cocktails with Lac des Battures lake as the backdrop.

• Strøm spa nordique, 1001 Boulevard de la Forêt, Nun's Island, stromspa.com

Be an elite diner
Earn 2X points on gas station, grocery store and dining purchases
The Air Canada Aeroplan® Card
Experience something elite.
Learn more at
Chase.com/AirCanadaCard
AIR CANADA AEROPLAN
CHASE
Mastercard, the circles design, World Mastercard and World Elite Mastercard are trademarks of Mastercard International Incorporated. Chase Air Canada Aeroplan Card credit cards are issued by JPMorgan Chase Bank, N.A. Member FDIC. Accounts subject to credit approval. Restrictions and limitations apply. Offer subject to change.

Culture

Curtain Call

From concert halls and historic theaters to independent cinema and creative studios, the cultural scene thrives on performances and artists who refuse to stay inside the lines.

Center Stage

Canada's largest performing arts complex boasts six concert halls and theaters. Since its curtain first rose in 1963, *Place des Arts* has hosted local institutions like the Orchestre symphonique de Montréal and the Opéra de Montréal alongside international dancers, comedians and global music stars. Its sprawling outdoor esplanade serves as the epicenter for the city's most famous gatherings, including the world-renowned Festival International de Jazz de Montréal. Connected to the city's bustling underground network, it stands as a year-round sanctuary where world-class creativity meets the everyday energy of the street.

- Place des Arts, 175 Sainte-Catherine Street West, Quartier des Spectacles, placedesarts.com

Off Script

Theatre Sainte-Catherine blends raunchy grit with sharp wit. The New International, founded in 2009, runs the province's longest-running English improv show, *Sunday Night Improv*, preceded each week by a free two-hour workshop at the theater that often doubles as a scouting session for future performers. On Mondays, *Les Lundis* offers the same format in French. While most venues in Montréal lean French or English, this theater stands out for its fully bilingual sketch and comedy productions.

• Theatre Sainte-Catherine, 264 Sainte-Catherine Street East, Quartier des Spectacles, theatresaintecatherine.com

Now Showing

Cinéma Moderne programs the kind of cinema that makes you want to clear your week. Restored classics, Québec productions, international arthouse cinema, filmmaker retrospectives and themed series sit alongside the occasional new release, all chosen with a curatorial eye that feels rare. The café-bar and terrace encourage arriving early, and latecomers aren't admitted, which tells you everything about how seriously the theater takes what's on screen. It's the type of place that makes going to the movies feel like an occasion again.

• Cinéma Moderne, 5150 Saint-Laurent Boulevard, Mile End, cinemamoderne.com

Deep End

Once a public swimming pool, *Bain Mathieu* has reinvented itself as one of the city's most genuinely eclectic cultural venues. The restored building—original tiled walls, soaring ceilings and a nonprofit at the helm—now plays host to everything from immersive performances and electronic raves to vintage markets, cabaret acts and drag shows. The calendar changes constantly, so check what's on before you go: You could end up at a life-drawing session one night and an all-night dance party the next. Either way, Bain Mathieu puts a whole new spin on the idea of a pool party.

• Bain Mathieu, 2915 Ontario Street East, Mercier-Hochelaga-Maisonneuve, bainmathieu.ca

Photos: Joseph Fuda, SPAG, Boris Laplante

Photo: Circo de Bakuza/Destination Montréal

From Montréal to the World

The dates and details may shift depending on who tells the story, but one thing seems certain: One of Montréal's top creative agencies began as a bohemian street show and interactive circus.

Circo de Bakuza—the name of the show and, later, the agency—found early success producing global events for Cirque du Soleil (also born in Montréal) and local productions for Bell Canada galas (photo) and Formula 1 Grand Prix parties. Its biggest break came in 2016 when the company was hired to produce 51 ceremonies for the UEFA European Football Championship in France, including the opening ceremony in Paris, where David Guetta performed the tournament's official anthem. From there, the agency was staging soccer ceremonies around the world, from the Africa Cup of Nations in Cairo to the World Cup in Qatar.

As European business grew, the agency established *Studio Bakuza*, a branding and design division focused on luxury brands. The studio opened its main office in Paris, with creative tech from Montréal, working with luxury houses like Jean-Paul Gaultier, Carolina Herrera and Prada. The experiential side then became *Bakuza Events*, with many more sporting events as well as brand activations like a Hublot party at Art Basel Miami Beach and a Comme des Garçons product launch in New York City. A third office has since opened in Barcelona.

It's a long way from the agency's beginnings as a street circus in the city. Probably not what anyone expected when someone first said, "Send in the clowns."

• Circo de Bakuza/Destination Montréal

Explore

Montréal

One Neighborhood at a Time

Montréal rewards slow travel. It's a city where a quick espresso easily stretches into an hour on a leafy terrace, a stop at the market becomes lunch, and the best moments are often the ones you never planned. Spend a weekend exploring its distinct districts, and you'll discover a city unlike anywhere else in North America.

Le Plateau-Mont-Royal

Old Port of Montréal

Start your morning in Mile End, where debating Montréal's legendary bagel shops is practically a local pastime. Grab a warm sesame bagel fresh from the wood-fired oven, then wander past independent bookstores, vintage boutiques and colorful street art. From there, head into neighboring Le Plateau-Mont-Royal to admire its iconic exterior spiral staircases and colorful Victorian homes. Browse local design shops before settling in at a neighborhood bistro for lunch. Whether sharing a few small plates or digging in for a multicourse lunch, paying with your Chase Air Canada Aeroplan® Card earns you 2X points at restaurants, turning one of the city's greatest pleasures into another step toward your next adventure.

After lunch, head north to *Jean-Talon Market*, one of Montréal's great public markets. It's a feast of Québec cheeses, seasonal produce and maple treats. As the afternoon unfolds, head south toward Griffintown, where former industrial warehouses have been converted into modern art galleries, craft breweries and stylish cafés along the historic Lachine Canal. Rent a cruiser for a ride along the waterfront before continuing east into Old Montréal, where the modern streets give way to centuries-old stone facades, cobblestone laneways and public plazas.

As dusk falls, Old Montréal comes alive. Wander through Place Jacques-Cartier, browse boutique galleries and settle into an acclaimed restaurant like *Monarque*. Finish the night with a cocktail at *The Coldroom* speakeasy or atop a rooftop bar like *Terrasse Nelligan* with views of the Old Port. From intimate wine bars to fine-dining institutions, the experience is less about checking attractions off a list than letting the city reveal itself at its own pace.

The magic of a Montréal weekend is that it always leaves you wanting more, and the Chase Air Canada Card helps pave the way for your next visit. Cardmembers earn up to 5X total points on Air Canada purchases and receive up to $100 in Air Canada statement credits annually. The card also awards automatic Elite Status with no minimum spend required, unlocking benefits like Priority Check-In, free first checked bags and Priority Boarding (Zone 2). After all, a smoother journey makes for a better getaway, inspiring you to explore more neighborhoods on every return visit.

Available exclusively to qualified individuals with a U.S. address, the Chase Air Canada Card helps make it easier to return to Montréal or set your sights on somewhere entirely new. With Air Canada's 180+ destinations and over 1,300 destinations across its 45+ global airline partners, the world is wide open.

Le Plateau-Mont-Royal

Scan or learn more at chase.com/aircanadacard

Editors' Picks

Old World, New Stuff

Roll with It

Dime has grown from a local skate crew into one of Canada's most influential streetwear brands. Swing by its Montréal flagship and take home a hoodie, tee or one of the label's colorful skate decks, equally at home on the pavement or your wall.

- Dime skate deck, dimemtl.com

Phone Home

For a Montréal fashion fix, check out the Arch Smooth Leather Phone Bag by *WANT Les Essentiels.* Made from smooth Italian leather and available in three colors, it combines a secure phone compartment, three card slots and a detachable crossbody strap in a compact bag-clutch hybrid.

- Arch Smooth Leather Phone Bag, wantlesessentiels.com

Maple Chocolate

Vegan and rich in antioxidants, this bean-to-bar dark chocolate adds pure maple sugar and a pinch of fleur de sel, balancing rich cacao flavor with the province's signature sweetness.

- Chocolate Noir, amangocacao.com

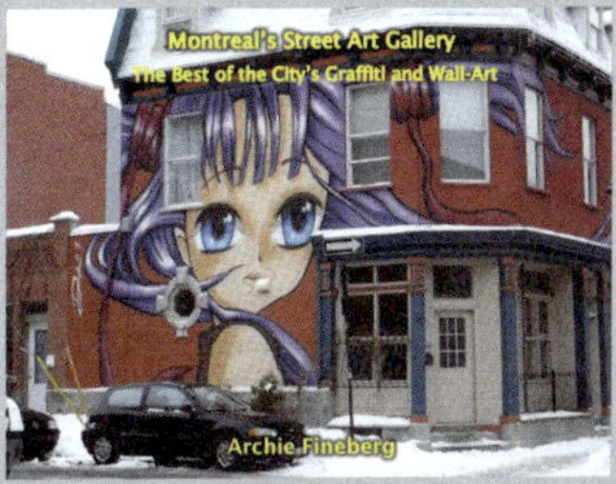

Read

Montréal's Street Art Gallery
• Archie Fineberg, 2017

Archie Fineberg spent years documenting Montréal's street galleries, collecting more than 140 photographs in this book. His subjects range from sanctioned murals and graffiti tags to the emerging art of yarn bombing. A second volume followed in 2022, proving the city's walls are always writing a new chapter.

The Apprenticeship of Duddy Kravitz
• Mordecai Richler, 1959

This sharp-edged novel follows a working-class Jewish teenager from the St. Urbain Street neighborhood as he schemes his way toward wealth and respectability. It's funny, fast-paced and morally questionable. Richard Dreyfuss starred in the Oscar-nominated film adaptation 15 years later.

The Tin Flute
• Gabrielle Roy, 1945

Before high-end restaurants and trendy boutiques, Saint-Henri was a working-class railway district. Set during the bleak winter of 1940, *Bonheur d'occasion* [The Tin Flute] follows Florentine Lacasse, a young waitress struggling to pull her family out of poverty as World War II looms. A global bestseller, the award-winning novel fueled social change and remains a landmark of Canadian literature.

Watch

C.R.A.Z.Y.
• Jean-Marc Vallée, 2005

Years before achieving global fame with *Dallas Buyers Club* and *Big Little Lies*, Montréal native Jean-Marc Vallée made this coming-of-age story about a young gay man growing up in Québec during the 1960s and 1970s. Primarily filmed in Montréal, the film stacked the soundtrack with David Bowie, Pink Floyd, Jefferson Airplane and the Rolling Stones.

Peace Park
• David Boots, 2013

When local skater and filmmaker David "Boots" Bouthillier began filming at Peace Park in 2001, he set out to capture Montréal's skate scene. Over the next decade, the footage evolved into a portrait of a city that's raw, chaotic, creative, troubled and fiercely communal. The film ultimately asks who gets to claim public space, and what happens when a city tries to take it back.

Jesus of Montréal
• Denys Arcand, 1989

This Oscar-nominated film follows a group of actors hired to modernize a church's passion play, only to find themselves drifting further and further from orthodoxy. Probably not the film to watch with your Catholic grandma, but its irreverent take on faith, art and modern life comes wrapped in a beautiful portrait of Montréal.

Spin

Funeral
• Arcade Fire, 2004

Arcade Fire's debut channels grief, nostalgia and youthful anxiety into soaring, cathartic songs like "Wake Up" and "Rebellion (Lies)." With its raw emotional intensity, *Funeral* helped put Montréal's music scene on the map and introduced one of indie rock's most important new voices.

"Everybody Knows"
• Leonard Cohen, 1988

Forever woven into the city's bohemian soul, Leonard Cohen turned poetry, desire and despair into songs of startling intimacy. While "Hallelujah" remains his most famous track, "Everybody Knows" represents Cohen at his most sardonic: a dark, swaggering catalog of corruption, hypocrisy and doomed romance.

99.9%
• Kaytranada, 2016

Haitian-born Montréal producer Kaytranada broke big with his 2016 debut, blending house, funk, hip-hop and R&B into something effortlessly danceable. Even if EDM isn't your thing, give "Lite Spots" a spin. Like *99.9%* itself, the track is packed with woozy, groove-heavy production that feels like a cool breeze on a crowded dance floor.